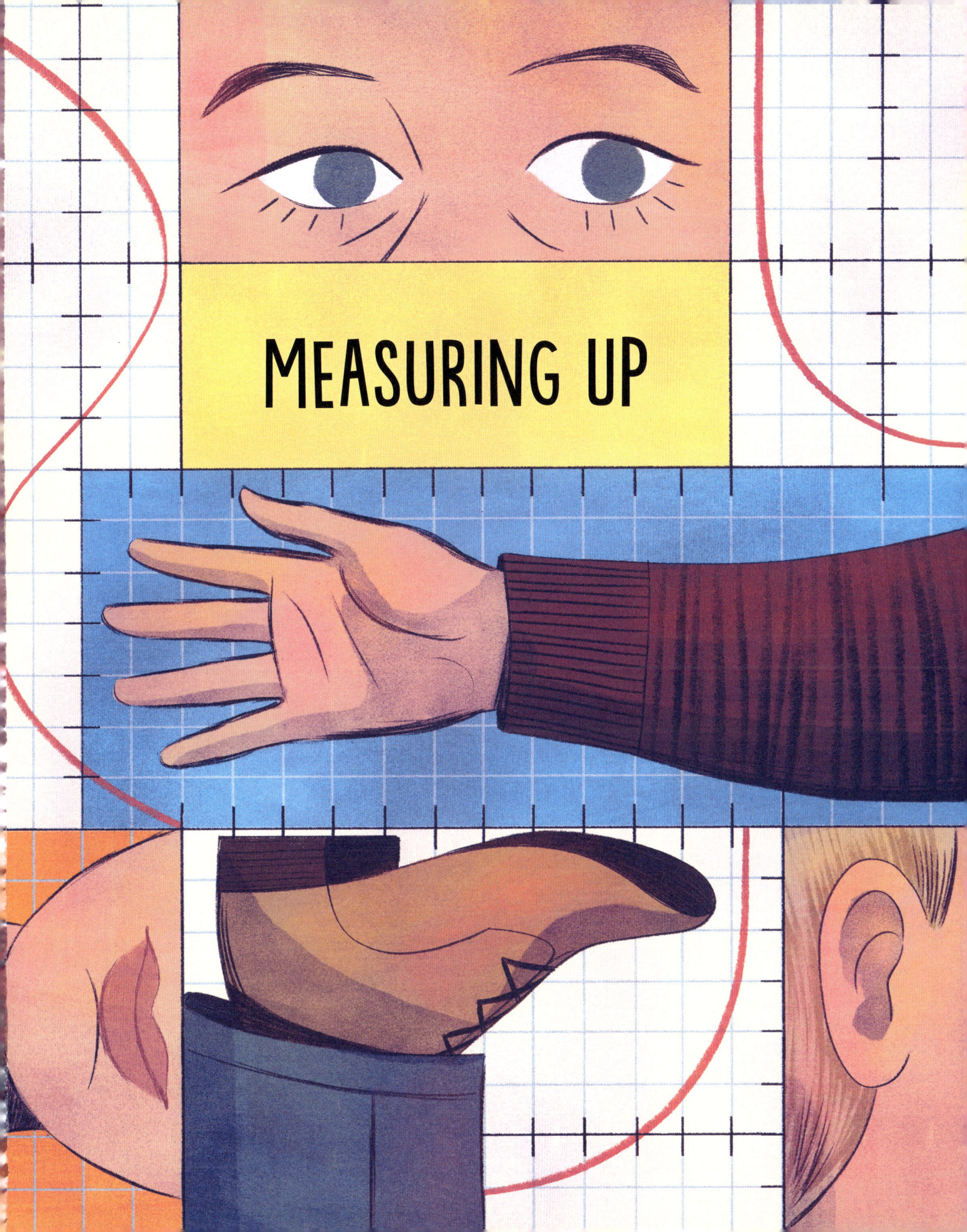

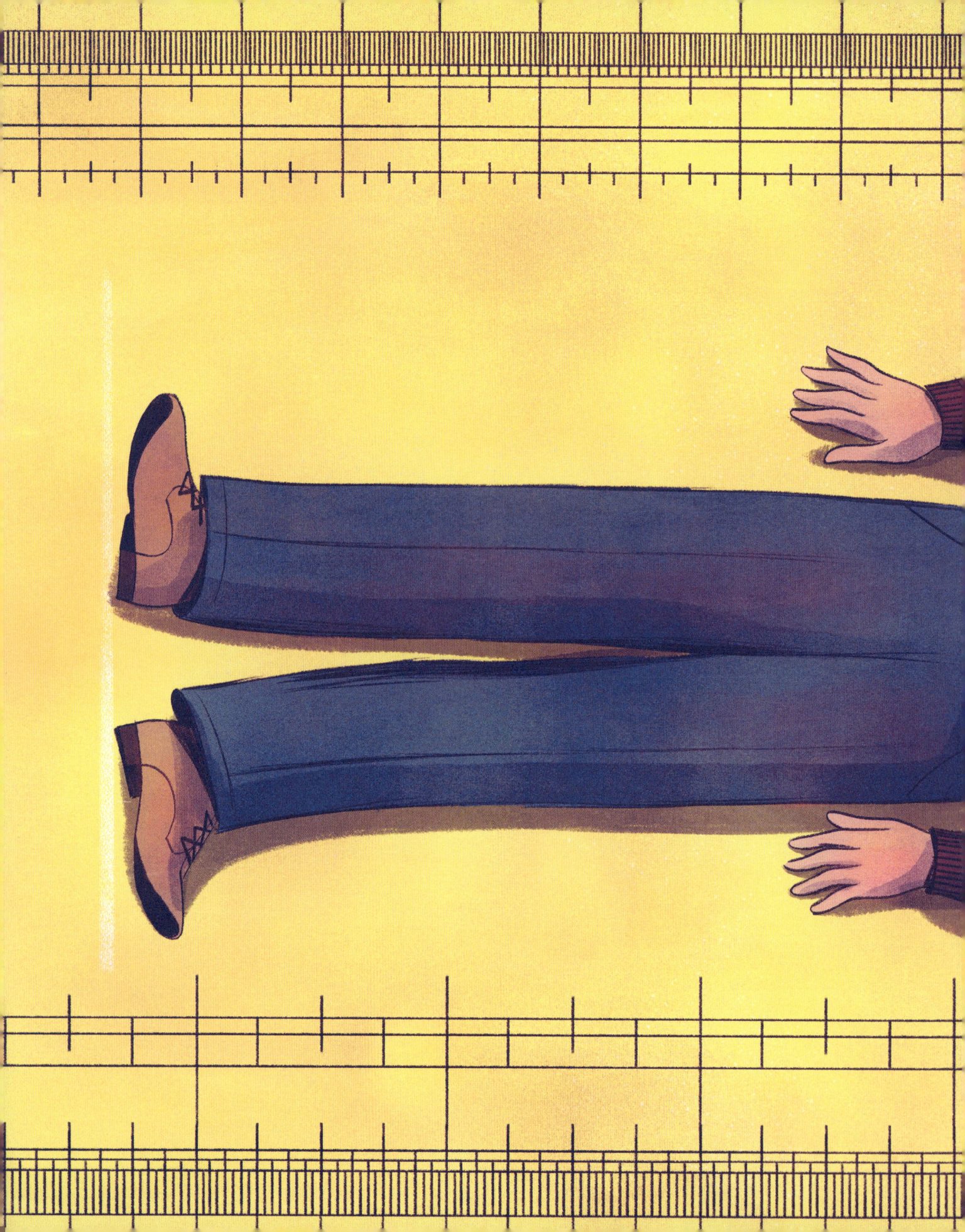

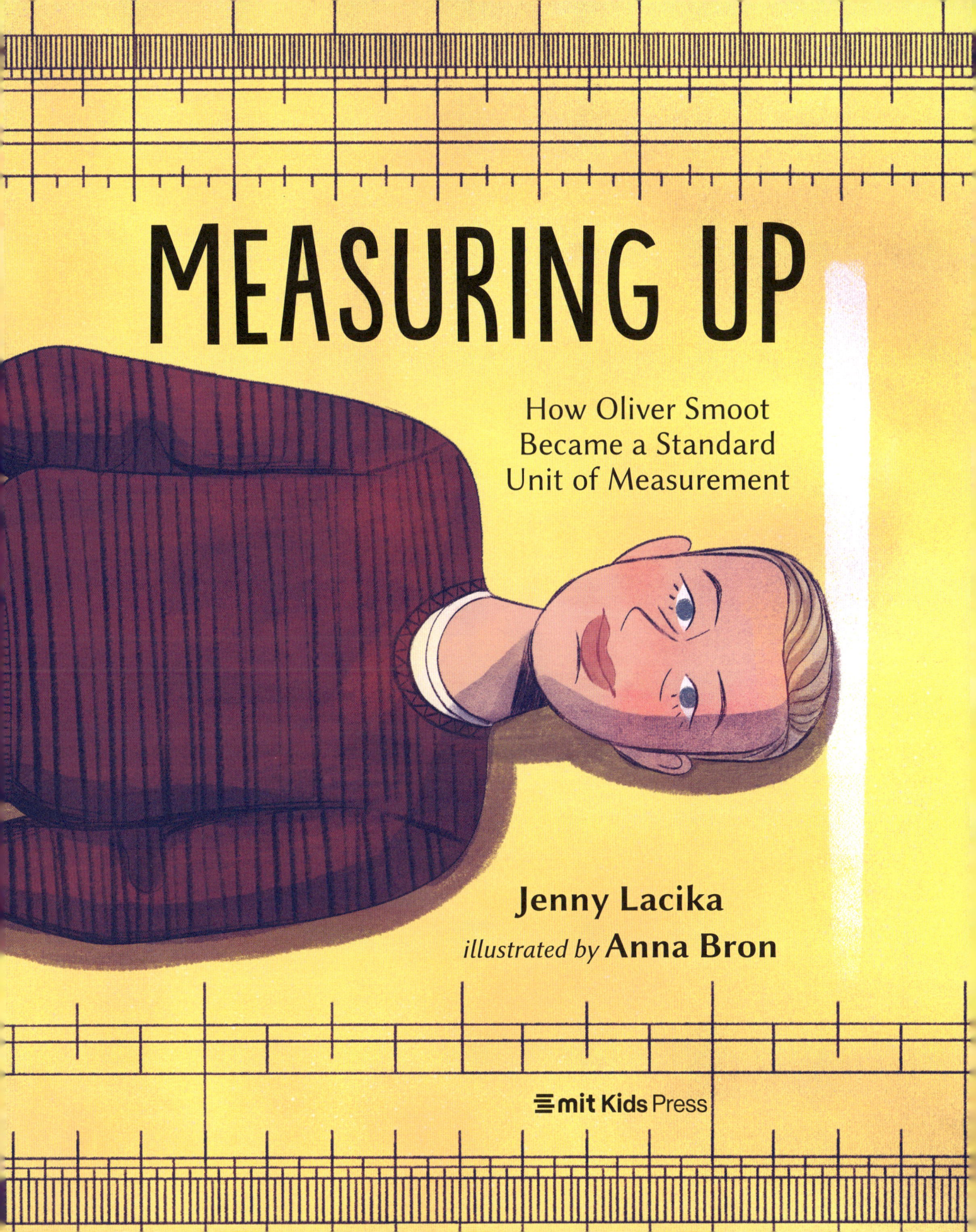

MEASURING UP

How Oliver Smoot Became a Standard Unit of Measurement

Jenny Lacika

illustrated by **Anna Bron**

ᴇmit Kids Press

Oliver "Ollie" Reed Smoot didn't measure up.

As fourteen friends gathered side by side to compare their heights, it was clear that he was the shortest.

And that's what he's famous for.

Freshmen at the Massachusetts Institute of Technology (MIT),
like Ollie, were immersed in numbers—from calculating and
quantifying in their calculus and physics classes to the
numbered buildings around them. They worked hard, but
they also had fun.

Ollie and his friends wanted to measure something big—the bridge that runs from Boston, Massachusetts, where they lived, over the Charles River where students like Ollie learned to sail, to the MIT campus in Cambridge.

But they didn't want to use a standard unit of measurement.

CHARLES

BOSTON

No ruler or yardstick or measuring tape or other object designed for measuring would do the trick.

They wanted to use a unit of measurement with a little more personality.

They also wanted a challenge, but what unit of measurement measured up to the task?

RIVER

MIT

OLLIE.

A SMOOT.

It even sounded scientific.
And so Ollie's journey from man to measurement began.

Ollie's friends measured him with a string, from head to foot, creating one smoot. They doubled and tripled the string until it was a few smoots long. The plan was to use this string over and over again to measure the bridge. Simple. Only it wasn't as simple as they thought.

The group wanted their efforts to stay a secret until their measurement was complete, so they gathered after sundown on a crisp October evening.

As they stretched the string straight and began marking the smoots, another friend stopped by to see how things were going. He was surprised.

They wanted a challenge. If they used a string, they might as well have used a measuring tape with standard units.

No character.

Ollie had to BE the measuring device.

But could he measure up to the task?

Ollie laid his body down, feet pointing to Boston. A friend marked his length with chalk. Ollie pushed himself up, walked down the bridge 5 feet 7 inches, and lay down again. Another mark.

Every ten smoots ended with a more permanent mark, made with weatherproof swimming pool paint.

Over and over again, Ollie pushed himself up to stand.
About 100 smoots in, he had done about 100 push-ups.
Ollie crossed this bridge almost every day, but never like this.
He was exhausted.

They weren't even halfway across the bridge,
but Ollie couldn't go on.
    Luckily, his friends were there to pick him up.

LITERALLY.

Heave ho! One smoot. Heave ho! Another smoot. Over and over, they moved Ollie down the cold concrete. Over and over, they marked the smoots.

About two-thirds of the way over the bridge, things were going pretty well.

Then, around smoot 300, they saw a van approach. The van slowed as it passed them, then made a U-turn.

The group scurried off the bridge and hid in the bushes between Buildings 1 and 2.

They didn't want to get caught. But they were determined to complete their task.

They waited.

When the coast was clear, they returned to their measurements.

About two hours and 364 smoots from when they first began, they were almost finished.

As the group laid Ollie down for the last time, more than half of his body extended past the end of the bridge.

They marked the final measurement:
364.4 smoots + 1 εar.

Ollie assumed their work would be quickly forgotten, but the story doesn't end there.

Every year, students repaint those marks made that night in 1958.

364.4 SMOOTS +1 EAR

In 1984, a plaque commemorating twenty-five years of smoots was installed. And promptly stolen.

Then the smoot came up against a real challenge to its legacy.

THE SMOOT

The bridge was reconstructed in the late 1980s.

 This could have been the end of the smoots, but they got an upgrade instead.

 Rather than scoring the sidewalk every six feet, as is standard, the contractor scored the sidewalk on every smoot.

 The smoot was now a permanent fixture on the bridge, cementing its place in history.

In 2008, a ceremony celebrating the smoot's fiftieth anniversary was held, and a second plaque was installed, this time more securely.

In 2011, the smoot was officially added to the *American Heritage Dictionary.*
And Ollie?

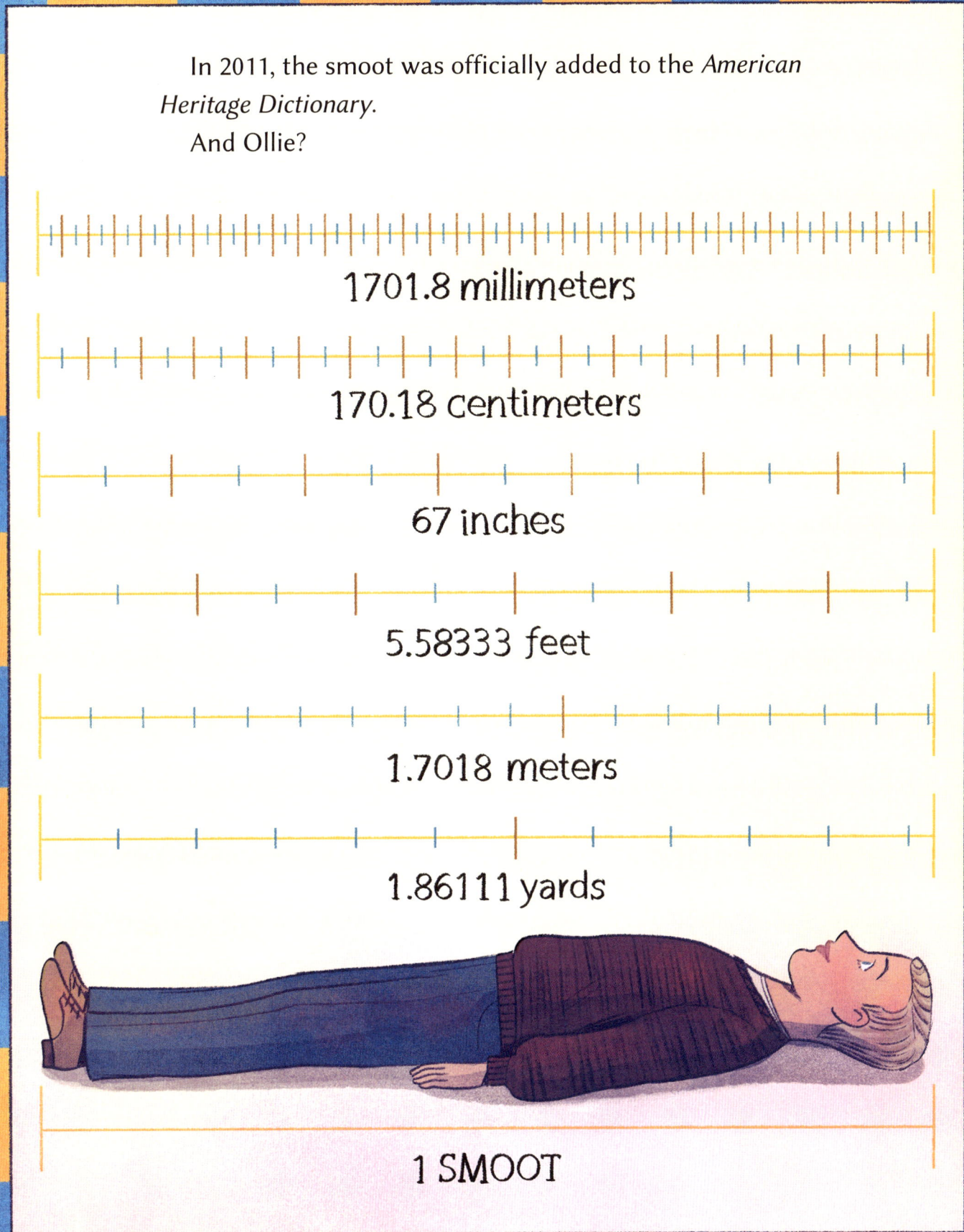

1701.8 millimeters

170.18 centimeters

67 inches

5.58333 feet

1.7018 meters

1.86111 yards

1 SMOOT

Ollie completed his economics degree in 1962.

After college, Ollie moved to Washington, DC, and became a lawyer.

Then he worked as a computer programmer.

Among his many professional successes are serving as chairman of the American National Standards Institute (ANSI) and president of the International Organization for Standardization (ISO), two organizations that make standards for measurement around the world.

Ollie becoming famous for his height seemed like a long shot. If he were half an inch taller, this story wouldn't be about him. But sometimes small acts can have BIG results.

Like the small act of lying down, something you probably do every evening. Ollie did it 365 times—a whole year of bedtimes in one night—growing his height into something bigger than himself.

When it comes to measurements, Ollie more than measures up.

MORE ABOUT SMOOTS

How did they get that 0.4 smoots?

When Oliver was lying down for the final measurement, his body extended past the end of the bridge. If Oliver's body were divided into 10 equal parts, 4 of the 10 parts would be on the bridge: $^4/_{10}$, or 0.4.

What does the εar mean?

Epsilon, ε, is used in mathematics to indicate a small uncertain quantity. When Oliver and his friends completed the measurement of the bridge, they knew that in measurement, it's possible to have some small variance due to human error. They included the + 1 εar to indicate this possible error. The measurement was later changed to ± 1 εar because it is possible to introduce error that results in a measurement that is too short or too long.

How far is your house from school in smoots?

Google will convert any distance into smoots. How many smoots from your home to your classroom? How many smoots from where you are now to the Harvard Bridge in Cambridge, Massachusetts?

HACKS: AN MIT TRADITION

Why exactly did Oliver Smoot and his friends want to measure the bridge with a nonstandard measurement? They were taking part in a long-standing MIT tradition of practical jokes, or "hacks." Hacks are designed to entertain the MIT community and often have an engineering twist.

Oliver's famous hack took little equipment. Just Oliver and some paint. Many other hacks required extensive planning and specialized equipment. Some other famous hacks include turning the Great Dome atop Building 10 into a giant R2-D2, assembling a replica of a campus police car on top of the dome, and turning the windows of the eighteen-floor Building 54, or Green Building, into a giant playable game of *Tetris*.

To learn more about the history of hacks at MIT:

MIT Hacks Gallery: http://hacks.mit.edu

Leibowitz, Brian M. *The Journal of the Institute for Hacks, Tomfoolery & Pranks at MIT.* Cambridge, MA: MIT Museum/MIT Press, 1990.

Peterson, T. F. *Nightwork: A History of Hacks and Pranks at MIT.* Updated ed. Cambridge, MA: MIT Press, 2011.

MORE MEASUREMENTS

Oliver Smoot is not the only person with his own unit of measurement. Some other people who invented or inspired unusual measurements include:

- ◆ **VIRGINIA APGAR**, an obstetric anesthesiologist, developed the Apgar score, a method to quickly assess the health of newborns based on their appearance, pulse, grimace, activity, and respiration (making for a good acronym that happens to also be her name!).

- ◆ **FRANCIS BEAUFORT**, a hydrographer, or scientist who studies the characteristics of bodies of water, developed the Beaufort wind force scale to describe wind conditions on land or sea.

- ◆ **JOHAN AUGUST BRINELL**, an engineer, developed the Brinell hardness scale by shooting tiny cannonballs into various metals.

- ◆ **MARIE AND PIERRE CURIE**, Nobel Prize–winning scientists, were the inspiration for the curie, a measure of radioactivity.

- ◆ **TETSUYA FUJITA**, a meteorology professor, developed the Fujita scale, a measure of tornado intensity.

- ◆ **JAKE GARN**, a US Senator and "citizen passenger" on a space shuttle flight, inspired the unofficial Garn scale, a measure of space sickness.

- ◆ **FRIEDRICH MOHS**, a geologist and mineralogist, classified minerals with the Mohs scale of mineral hardness.

- ◆ **JUSTIN O. SCHMIDT**, an entomologist, or biologist who studies insects, created the Schmidt sting pain index for insect stings by intentionally stinging himself with a variety of insects and rating the pain he felt.

- ◆ **WILBUR SCOVILLE**, a pharmacist, created the Scoville scale to measure the spiciness of chili peppers by tasting and rating the different varieties.

BIBLIOGRAPHY

Arthur, Benjamin, and Robert Krulwich. "What's a Smoot?" *Krulwich Wonders*, NPR, October 5, 2011.

Brehm, Denise. "Keyser Describes His Top Five Hacks." *MIT News*, September 1, 1999.

Durant, Elizabeth. "Smoot's Legacy: 50th Anniversary of Famous Feat Nears." *MIT Technology Review*, June 23, 2008.

Duvergne Smith, Nancy. "'Smoot' Enters the Dictionary." *Slice of MIT*, November 22, 2011.

Geeslin, Ned, and S. Avery Brown. "With a Campus Legend in Peril, Members of a Fraternity Vow to Save the Endangered M.I.T. Smoot." *People*, April 24, 1989, 93–95.

Gillooly, Patrick. "Smoot Reflects on His Measurement Feat as 50th Anniversary Nears." *MIT News*, September 24, 2008.

London, Jay. "Smoot Lighting to Set the Mood on Harvard Bridge." *Slice of MIT*, October 21, 2014.

Lyons, Ana. "Plaque Shows Off Alum Smoot's Contribution to Measurement." *The Tech*, June 5, 2009.

Marcott, Amy. "New Smoot Plaque Greets Mass. Ave. Bridge Crossers." *Slice of MIT*, June 4, 2009.

"MIT Celebrates the 50th Smoot-aversary." Smoot Celebration Day, October 4, 2008, website.

Moyer, Ilan E. "50th Anniversary Smoot Plaque." Ilan E. Moyer, MIT online portfolio.

"Ollie Smoot, the Official Unit of Measure for the Harvard Bridge." *Radio Boston*, WBUR, May 6, 2016.

"Smoot, Namesake of a Unit of Length, Retires." *All Things Considered*, NPR, December 7, 2005.

Smoot, Oliver. Email correspondence with author. July 6, 2022. October 24, 2022.

Tavernor, Robert. *Smoot's Ear: The Measure of Humanity*. New Haven, CT: Yale University Press, 2007.

To OGP
JL

To Mom and Dad
AB

The MIT Press, the ☰mit Kids Press colophon, and MIT Kids Press are trademarks of The MIT Press, a department of the Massachusetts Institute of Technology, and used under license from The MIT Press. The colophon and MIT Kids Press are registered in the US Patent and Trademark Office.

First edition 2025

Library of Congress Catalog Card Number pending
ISBN 978-1-5362-3012-3

25 26 27 28 29 30 CCP 10 9 8 7 6 5 4 3 2 1

Printed in Shenzhen, Guangdong, China

This book was typeset in Linux Biolinum.
The illustrations were created digitally.

MIT Kids Press
an imprint of Candlewick Press
99 Dover Street
Somerville, Massachusetts 02144

mitkidspress.com
candlewick.com

EU Authorized Representative: HackettFlynn Ltd., 36 Cloch Choirneal, Balrothery, Co. Dublin, K32 C942, Ireland. EU@walkerpublishinggroup.com

JENNY LACIKA is a graduate of MIT and the author of the Mathical Book Prize winner *Again, Essie?*, illustrated by Teresa Martínez. As a student, she crossed the bridge between Boston and Cambridge countless times. She measures about 0.96 smoots in length and now lives over 2 million smoots away from the bridge, in New Mexico. You can visit her online at www.jennylacika.com.

ANNA BRON is the illustrator of *The Five Sides of Marjorie Rice: How to Discover a Shape* by Amy Alznauer, *Wild at Heart: The Story of Olaus and Mardy Murie, Defenders of Nature* by Evan Griffith, *No Horses in the House! The Audacious Life of Artist Rosa Bonheur* by Mireille Messier, and the Salma series by Danny Ramadan. She also works as an animation director on commercials and short films, one of which was nominated for an Oscar, another for an Emmy. Anna Bron lives in Canada.

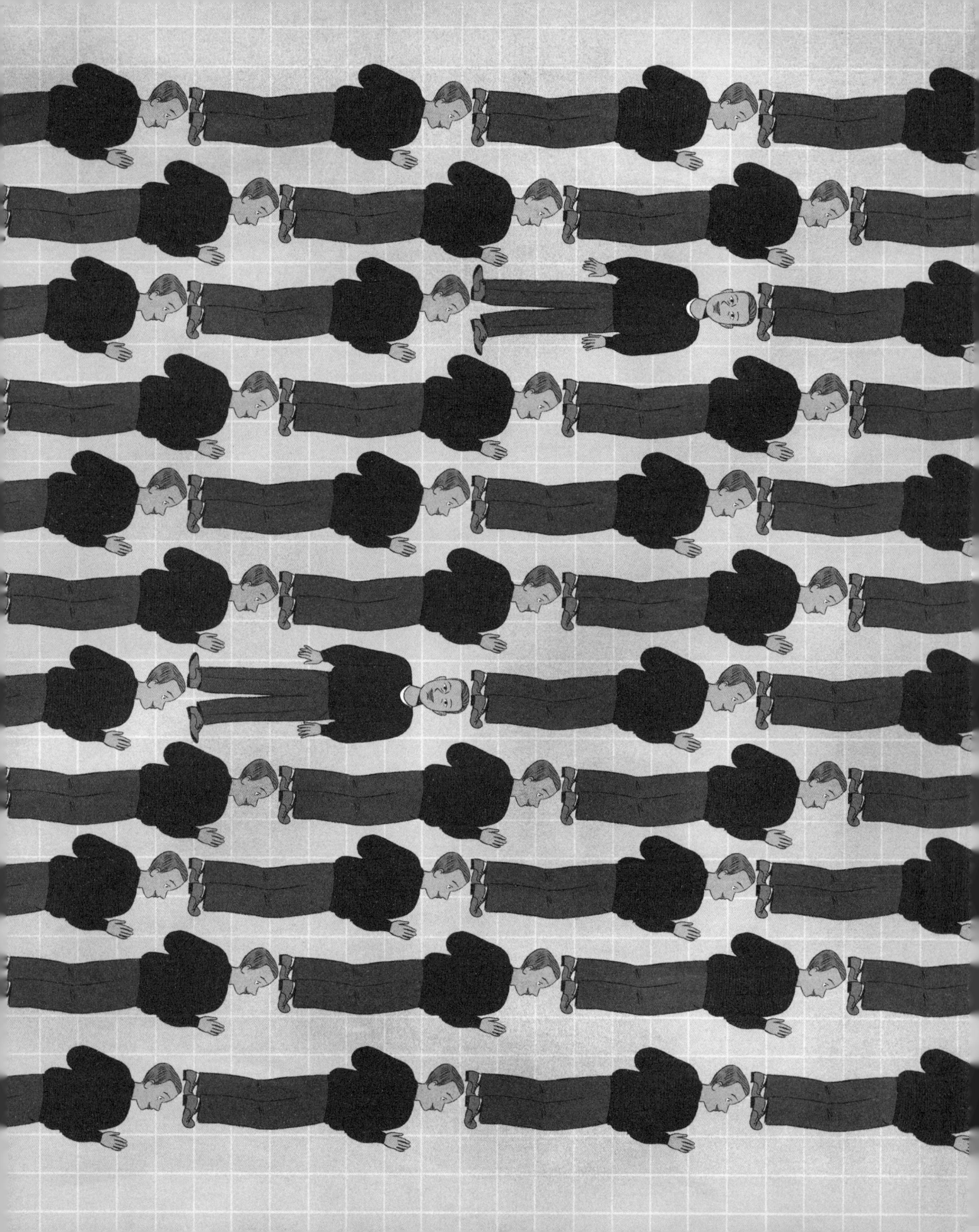